THIS BOOK
BELONGS TO

YOUR OPINION MATTERS!

★ ★ ★ ★ ★

Thank you for purchasing.
If you enjoyed this book,
we would appreciate
your positive feedback and review.

Cheers!

For ordering customize book, please visit:

www.posondo.com/book

YOUR OPINION MATTERS!

★ ★ ★ ★ ★

Thank you for purchasing.
If you enjoyed this book,
we would appreciate
your positive feedback and review.

Cheers!

For ordering customize book, please visit:

www.posondo.com/book

Made in the USA
Monee, IL
20 September 2023

43071129R00070